Amelia Pickering

The Sorrows of Werter

A Poem

Amelia Pickering

The Sorrows of Werter
A Poem

ISBN/EAN: 9783744712637

Printed in Europe, USA, Canada, Australia, Japan

Cover: Foto ©Thomas Meinert / pixelio.de

More available books at **www.hansebooks.com**

THE

SORROWS OF WERTER:

A

POEM.

THE

SORROWS of WERTER:

A

P O E M.

BY

A M E L I A   P I C K E R I N G.

———————

HERE LIES A YOUTH BORNE DOWN WITH LOVE AND CARE;
HE COULD NOT LONG HIS DELIA'S LOSS ABIDE:
JOY LEFT HIS BOSOM WITH THE PARTING FAIR;
AND WHEN HE DURST NO LONGER HOPE—HE DIED.

HAMMOND.

———————

L O N D O N:

PRINTED FOR T. CADELL, IN THE STRAND.

M.DCC.LXXXVIII.

TO THE

R E A D E R.

SHOULD some sweet nymph, perhaps, as Charlotte fair,

Read, without scorn, these pages of despair;

Some happier Werter give the vacant hour,

To mark the woes of Love's destructive power;

Ah! let them pause on this display of woe:

O'er Werter's sorrows Pity's tears should flow:

Ah! let them pause on this distressful tale:

O'er Werter's errors draw Oblivion's veil;

Remember'd but to mark the fatal end,

Where Love's ungovern'd paffions blindly tend:

To curb impatience; better hopes impart;

And point the moral to the feeling heart.

Though Honour plac'd in Werter's heart her throne;.

Though weeping Virtue mark'd him for her own;

Nor Virtue's fhield, nor Honour's arm could fave,

Love's wretched victim from an early grave.

SUBSCRIBERS.

A.

EARL of Abingdon.
Countefs of Abingdon.
Countefs of Albemarle.
Samuel Atkins, Efq. Wickham, Hants.
Mrs. Atkins.
Mr. Atkins.
Mr. Agar.
Mrs. J. Allen, Greenwich.
Mr. Allen.
Mrs. Alcock, Little Chelfea.
Mr. Serjeant Adair.
Mrs. Adair.
Mrs. Adair, Portugal-Street.
Mifs Adair, Southampton-Row.
William Adair, Efq. Lincoln's-Inn.
Henry Atherton, Efq.
George Edward Allen, Efq.
——— Angerftein, Efq.
A. A.
Henry Addington, Efq.
Charles Ambler, Efq.
Mrs. Abdy.
Mifs Arnold.
Mrs. Adean.

Francis Annefley, Efq.
Martin Annefley, Efq.
Mrs. Annefley.
Mifs Annefley.
Mrs. Ambler.
Anonymous, a Lady.
Anonymous, a Gentleman.
——— Agar, Efq.
Dr. Afh.
Mifs Afhley.
Mrs. Atwood.
Mrs. Aversfield.
Chriftopher Anftey, Efq.
Mrs. Anftey.
Rev. Mr. Anftey.
Benjamin Afhe, Efq.
Mr. A. Auckey.
Alexander Adair, Efq.
Mrs. Adair.
Sir William Afhurft.
Lady Afhurft.

B.

Dutchefs of Bolton.
Rt. Hon. Lord Boyle.
Rt. Hon. Lord Bayham.

Richard

Richard Barwell, Efq. ·
Mrs. Mary Barwell, Ormond-Street.
Mifs Sarah Blackwood, Clifton.
Shovel Blackwood, Efq. Black-
heath.
Mrs. Blackwood.
Mifs Blackwood.
Mifs Catherine Blackwood.
Mrs. Charles Brett.
Mrs. Baker, Bedford-Square.
Mrs. Blake.
Mrs. Blackman.
Mrs. Elizabeth Blackman.
Mifs Benfon.
———— Bell, Efq.
Mrs. Bell.
Alexander Bennet, Efq.
Mrs. Bennet.
Mifs Bull.
Mifs C. Bull.
Mr. Bunn.
Mr. B. Bunn.
Mr. J. Bunn.
Mr. T. Bunn.
———— Boyfield, Efq.
Mrs. Boyfield, Lee.
Mifs Boyfield.
Mifs E. Boyfield.
Mifs B. Boyfield.
Rev. Dr. Burnaby, Greenwich.
Mifs A. M. Bentley, Abingdon-
Street.
Thomas Bernard, Efq.
Mrs. Bernard.

Charles Butler, Efq. Ormond-
Street.
Mrs. Barnard.
Mifs Badcock.
Mifs F. Badcock.
Mrs. Braham.
George Briftow, Efq.
Timothy Brown, Efq.
Mr. Brichwood.
Lady Blunt, Ormond-Street.
Mrs. D. Blunt, Kew.
James Blunt, Efq.
Mrs. Blair.
Mifs Jane Blair.
Mrs. Burrell.
William Burrell, Efq.
Lady Charlotte Bertie.
Lady Boyd.
Mifs Boyd.
John Boyd, Efq.
Mrs. Boyd.
Mrs. Bates.
Mifs Blackman.
Mifs Bloffet.
Mrs. Banks.
———— Banks, Efq.
William Bumpfted, Efq.
A Lady by ditto.
Dr. Budd.
Francis Bofanquet, Efq.
William Bofanquet, Efq.
Earl of Barrymore.
Rt. Hon. ———— by ditto.
Lady Carolina Barry.

Hon,

[ix]

Hon. Henry Barry.
Hon. Auguſtus Barry.
Mrs. Blount.
Iſaac Hawkins Brown, Eſq.
Miſs Baker.
Mrs. Brocas.
William Black, Eſq.
Eliſha Briſcoe, Eſq.
Edward Gale Boldero, Eſq..
Mrs. Blandy.
Miſs Blandy.
Miſs Mary Blandy..
Mr. J. Blandy.
Mrs. Bulley.
Miſs Bulley.
Miſs Brouncker.
Mrs. Brockman..
Miſs Brockman.
Miſs S. Brockman.
Mr. James Brockman;.
James Drake Brockman, Eſq.
——— Beardſworth, Eſq.
Mrs. Biſcoe..
Mrs. Beauvoir.
Iſaac Bargrave, Eſq.
Mrs. Broadley.
Dr. Boulton.
Henry Boulton, jun..
Mrs. Brabazon.
H. H. Brown, Eſq.
John Brathwaite, Eſq..
William Biſhop, Eſq.
Lady Blois.
Rev. Philip Baker.

John Barlow, Eſq.
Mr. Blackſtone.
Mrs. Buller, Wincheſter.
Miſs Buller.
Mrs. Blackwell.
Rev. Mr. Bargus..
Mrs. Blackſtone..
Miſs Blackſtone.
Miſs P. Blackſtone..
Mr. Bax..
John Bathor, Eſq.
C. W. Bamfylde, Eſq..
Mrs. Blair..
Edward Barnard, Eſq..
James Burn, Eſq.
Miſs Burn.
Miſs J. Burn.
Edward Boodle, Eſq..
Mrs. Burrell.
John Bland, Eſq.
Benjamin Barnett, Eſq.
Samuel Beachcroft, Eſq..
Barrington Buggin, Eſq..
Miſs Brown..
James Bradſhaw, Eſq.
Mrs. Brown, Chancery-Lane.
Henry Barker, Eſq. Gray's-Inn..

C.

Lord Frederick Campbell..
Lady Clive.
Stephen Cottrell, Eſq..
Mrs. Cottrell.
Miſs Cartwright..

Miſs

Mifs Eliza Cartwright.
Mifs Charlotte Cartwright.
John Cator, Efq.
Mrs. Cator.
Jofeph Cator, Efq.
Mrs. W. Cator.
D. Crefpin, Efq. Clifton.
Mrs. Chapman.
Thomas Collins, Efq.
Mifs Crofts.
Philip Cade, Efq.
Richard Cox, Efq.
Mifs Cox.
Lady Carr.
Mifs Carr.
Mifs Chowne.
Mrs. Caftle.
Rev. Dr. Courtenay.
Lady E. Courtenay.
C. F. Cazenave, Efq.
Mr. Cox.
Charles Alexander Crickitt, Efq.
Robert Henry Crew, Efq.
Mr. Colmas.
Mifs Elizabeth Crofts.
Mr. Clay.
Mr. F. Clay.
Mifs Caters, Bath.
Mrs. Carter.
Afhley Cowper, Efq.
Mifs Cowper.
Mrs. S. Caufton.
—— Caufton, Efq.
Mifs Caufton.
—— Cray, Efq.

Mrs. Cray.
Henry Cowper, Efq.
Mrs. H. Cowper.
Thomas Chapman, Efq.
Mrs. Clarke.
Mrs. Coventry.
Thomas Colborne, Efq.
Oliver Cromwell, Efq.
Mrs. Clements.
Rev. Mr. Clarke.
—— Clifford, Efq.
—— Cooper, Efq. Southampton-
   Buildings.
Robert Church, Efq.
Mrs. Chace.
Mr. Cadell.
Rev. Mr. Cromleholme.
Mrs. Cromleholme.
Rev. Dr. Chelfum.
Mifs Croffweller.
Mr. J. Clarke.
Hon. Mr. Chichefter.
Mr. Carey.
Mifs Cafmajor.
Mifs Colleton.
Mifs Cotes.
Mrs. Cotterell.
Timothy Curtis, Efq.
Rev. H. I. Clofe.
William Curtis, Efq.
Thomas Colborne, Efq.
Jacob Crofts, Efq. King's Bench
   Walks.
Mrs. Carn.

Earl

D.

Earl of Dartmouth.
Countess of Dartmouth.
Bishop of Durham.
Mr. T. Dickens.
Mrs. Davics, Comb-Grove.
Mr. Dyer.
Mrs. Dickenson.
Mr. De Mousieur.
Richard Dowding, Esq.
Richard Dickenson, Esq.
Mrs. Denis, Percy-Street.
Major Darby.
Captain John Darby.
The Rev. Mr. Dodwell.
Miss Davison.
Henry Dean, Esq.
Mrs. Dean.
John Deverell, Esq. Clifton.
Richard Blake Deverell, Esq.
Miss Deverell.
Master George Frederic Deverell.
Charles Deaves, Esq.
William Deeds, jun. Esq.
William Dickens, Esq.
William Dickens, jun. Esq.
Charles Dornford, Esq.
Robert Dent, Esq.
Mr. John Dent.
Mr. Donnaldson.
Mrs. Drake.
Charles Delaft, Esq.
Lady Davis.
Mrs. Demainbray.

———— D'Oyley, Esq.
Mr. Darell.
Mr. R. Darell.
Mr. Dundass.
Thomas Dew, Esq.
Sir John Durbin.
Lady Durbin.
Thomas Dumaresque, Esq.
William Dumaresque, Esq.
Rev. Richard Davis.
Mr. Dewell.
Mrs. Draper.
Rev. Mr. Dobson.
Rev. Mr. D'Oyley.
Robert Drummond, Esq.
Henry Drummond, Esq.
Andrew Drummond, Esq.
Henry Drummond, jun. Esq.
Charles Drummond, Esq.

E.

Miss Ewer.
Mrs. Elliot, Blackheath.
Richard Emmett, Esq.
Samuel Enderby, Esq.
Charles Enderby, Esq.
Samuel Enderby, jun. Esq.
———— Edison, Esq.
Mrs. Edison.
Rev. George Thomas Edison.
Mr. John Edison.
Miss Edison.
Mrs. Elton.
Miss Elton.

Lady

Lady Efdaile.
Peter Efdaile, Efq.
John Efdaile, Efq.
Mrs. W. Efdaile.
Rev. Mr. Edifon.
Samuel Eftwick, Efq.
Mrs. Eames.
A Lady by ditto.
Ditto by ditto.
T. H. Earle, Efq.
Mrs. Earle.
Mrs. Ekins.
M. E.
Thomas Eftcourt, Efq.
Mr. Edgar.
Mr. Ellitt.
Henry Earle, Efq.
Lady Eaft.
Mifs Elton.
William Evelyn, Efq.

F.

Applew-haite Frere, Efq.
Sir William Fitz-Herbert, Bart.
Lady Fitz-Herbert.
Anthony Fitz-Herbert, Efq.
Hon. Mifs Fox.
Mr. French.
Mrs. French.
Mrs. Frith.
R. Frewin, Efq.
J. F.
Mifs C. Fonnereau.
Mifs M. Fonnereau.

Mrs. Franklin.
Mrs. Fifher.
Philip Francis, Efq.
Mifs Furlow.
John Furlow, Efq.
Mrs. Farrell, Bath.
Mifs Farren, Bromley.
Mifs Foot.
William Fauquier, Efq. Stratton-
   Street.
Mifs Fauquier.
William Fauquier, Efq. Conduit-
   Street.
Mrs. Frampton.
The Rev. Mr. Foyle.
Mrs. Fanfhaw.
Stephen Flery, Efq.
Mrs. Forfter.
Mifs Forfter.
John Forfter, Efq.
Mr. John Forfter.
Mrs. Anne Francklin.
John Francklin, Efq.
Sir M. B. Folkes.
Lady Folkes.
Oliver Farrer, Efq.
Mrs. Fuller.
Mrs. Fullerton, Richmond.
Mr. John Francklin.
Mifs Francklin.
Mifs Foote.
Mrs. Francklin.
—— Frewin, Efq.
Mrs. Forfter.

3

W. Flower, Efq.
———— Finney, Efq.
Mrs. Finney.
The Rev. Mr. Foley.
T. Fauquier, Efq.
James Farquharfon, Efq.
Mifs Finch.
Mrs. Fell, Lincoln's-Inn-Fields.

G.

James Garth, Efq.
Mrs. Godin.
Mrs. Guftheart, Bath.
George Garnier, Efq. Wickham, Hants.
Mrs. Garnier.
Jofeph Grote, Efq.
Mrs. Garnault.
Mrs. Griffith.
Hon. Mrs. Levefon Gower.
Mr. Gift.
Mr. Glenny.
Mrs. George Grant, Piccadilly.
Mifs Guy, Lewifham.
Robert Gofling, Efq.
Mrs. Gofling.
Bertie Greathead, Efq.
Auguftus Greenland, Efq.
The Rev. Mr. Gamet.
Lady Gould.
Mifs Gibfon, Whitchurch.
Rev. Mr. Gray.
Lady Gatehoufe.
Thomas Graham, Efq.

James Graham, Efq.
George Griffin, Efq.
Charles Gwilt, Efq.
Mrs. Gundry.
Mifs Gundry.
Mr. N. Gundry.
Mrs. N. Gundry.
———— Gale, Efq.
Mrs. Gell, Hopton, Derbyfhire.
Carew Gauntlett, Efq. Winchefter.
Mifs Godwin.
Mifs Greenhill.
Mr. Gleede.
Sir William Gibbons, Bart.
S. Kenrick Gibbons, Efq.
David Gordon, Efq.
Mrs. Goidet.

H.

The Dutchefs of Hamilton.
Earl of Harcourt.
Countefs of Harcourt.
Mrs. Hotchkis.
Mrs. Horne.
Mifs Horne.
Mifs Elizabeth Horne.
Richard Hulfe, Efq.
William Hagen, Efq.
Jofeph Hethrington, Efq.
Mrs. Holland.
Mrs. Hyde.
Rev. Dr. Hamilton.
Lady Hoare.
Mrs. G. Hawker.

b

Mrs.

Mrs. Hodgkinfon.

Mrs. Hamilton, Greenwich.

John Holliday, Efq. Ormond-Street.

T. Hicks, Efq.

Mrs. Hicks.

Mifs Hicks.

Mifs R. Hicks.

John Heylyn, Efq.

Mrs. Hood.

Mr. Hollift.

Sir Benjamin Hammett.

Mrs. Hammett.

Mifs Hammett.

Mifs Eliza Hammett.

John Hammett, Efq.

John Hett, Efq.

Mrs. Hawkfworth, Bromley.

Mrs. Hales, Cottlis-Houfe, Wilts.

Peter Holford, Efq.

Mrs. Holford.

Mifs Holford.

Mifs Charlotte Holford.

Charles Grave Hudfon, Efq.

Mifs Hudfon.

Jofeph Hill, Efq.

Mrs. Hill.

Mrs. T. Hill.

Mrs. F. Hill.

Lady Hefketh.

Mrs. Holder.

William Hayley, Efq.

Mrs. Hanay.

Mifs Hayes.

The Rev. James Hayes.

Charles Hayes, Efq.

Henry Holland, Efq.

Mrs. Holland.

Robert Batefon Harvey, Efq.

John Hallett, Efq.

James Hallett, Efq.

Mifs Hallett.

Mifs Elizabeth Hallett.

Samuel Hoare, Efq.

John Hodges, Efq.

Richard Holland, Efq.

Andrews Harrifon, Efq.

John Harrifon, Efq.

Sir Richard Heron, Bart.

Mrs. Highmore.

Mrs. Hammond.

Henry L. Hunter, Efq.

Edward Hillyard, Efq.

Rev. Mr. Hodgkinfon.

Thomas Howard, Efq.

Edward Hillyard, for a Friend.

Nathaniel Howard, Efq.

Mifs Elizabeth Howard.

Mrs. Herring.

William Hamilton, Efq.

J. Harvey, Efq.

Captain Honeywood.

Mrs. Honeywood.

Mr. Haffan.

The Rev. Mr. Haggitt.

Mr. Hales, Cottlis-Court.

Mrs. Hewith.

———— Hales, Efq.

W. Hankins, Efq.

7

P. Hankins, Efq.
J. Hankins, Efq.
James Holder, Efq.
Mrs. Heyfham.

I.

Thomas Clerke Jervoife, Efq.
Mrs. Jackfon.
Mifs Jackfon.
Mifs E. Jackfon.
Godfchall Johnfon, Efq.
The Hon. William Henry Irby.
Mrs. Jenkins, Bath.
Mr. Ind.
Mrs. Ibbetfon.
Mrs. Jobbins.
A. J.
S. J.
Mr. Jones.
The Rev. Mr. Johnes, Stratford-
  Place.
Thomas Ingram, Efq.
Henry Jackfon, Efq.
Mrs Jefferys.
Mrs. Johnfon, Mortlake.
Arthur Jones, Efq.
Mrs. Jennings.
Mifs Jennings.
Robert Jenner, Efq.
John Ibbetfon, Efq.
Thomas Jordan, Efq.
George Jackfon, Efq.
Mrs. Jones.
Mrs. Jukes.
Lafcelles Iremonger, Efq.

K.

Mrs. King.
Mrs. Kerby.
Mr. K.
Mr. A. Kirwan.
Mr. King.
Mrs. Kearney.
Mifs Knight.
Colonel Kingfton.
Mrs. Knapp.
Mr. John Keyfall.
The Rev. Mr. Kipling.
Mr. J. Kipling.
Mrs. Knott.
Nathaniel Kemp, Efq.
Godfrey Kettle, Efq.

L.

Lady Lovaine.
Lord Leflie.
The Hon. Mrs. Leigh.
Rev. William Lowth, Prebendary
  of Winchefter.
Mr. William Latham, Eltham.
Mrs. William Latham.
A Lady in Spring-Gardens.
Heneage Legge, Efq.
Mrs. Legge.
Mrs. Larpent.
Edward Lacon, Efq.
Mrs. Lowth.
Mifs Lowth.
Mrs. L.
Sir William Lee.
Lady Elizabeth Lee.

Mrs.

Mrs. Luther, Grofvenor-Street.
Mifs Lewis.
Mifs Loveday.
Mrs. Mary Liell.
The Rev. Dr. Lynch.
The Rev. Mr. Lynch.
Mr. Links.
C. L.
Mifs Lowther.
Mr. Lifle.
Mrs. Lee.
Mrs. Long.
Mrs. Lunmore.
Beefton Long, Efq.
Nicholas Leach, Efq.
Rev. Robert Lowth.
Mrs. Ludby, Harley-Street.

M.

Duke of Manchefter.
Dowager Vifcountefs Montague.
Lord Montague.
The Hon. Mrs. Moore.
The Hon. Mrs. Mairn.
Mrs. Montague.
Matthew Montague, Efq.
Mrs. M. Montague.
Mrs. Middleton.
Captain Nicholas Maria Marchetti.
Lady Miller.
Mifs Miller.
Mifs M. Miller.
Mr. W. Myddleton, Temple.
Dowager Lady Miller.

Mrs. Melife.
Mr. Marfh.
General Maxwell.
Mifs Margaret Metcalf, Briftol.
Mifs Jane Metcalf.
John Mortlock, Efq.
Mrs. Mortlock.
Mifs Maaffree, Percy-Street.
Mr. John Meyer.
General Martin.
Mrs. Merlot, Briftol.
Mifs Merlot.
Mrs. Mellifh.
Mrs. Michelfen.
Mrs. Mabbott.
Lady Marfh.
Mrs. Martin.
Mrs. Micklem.
Mr. Montagu.
Mr. Benjamin Morland.
Mrs. Michell.
Mrs. Matthews, Reading.
John Marfh, Efq.
Robert Mackenzie, Efq.
Charles Monro, Efq.
James Mansfield, Efq.
George Milner, Efq.
—— Martin, Efq.
John Madocks, Efq.
Mrs. Madocks.
Mrs. Macartney.
William Melmoth, Efq. Bath.
Mrs. Martlett.
Mifs Martlett.

Mifs

[xvii]

Mifs M. Metcalf, Saville-Row.
Mifs J. Metcalf.
Langford Millington, Efq.
Henry Maxwell, Efq.
Mrs. Maxwell.
Mrs. Maltby.
Mr. Moore.
Mr. Mouch.
Jofeph Martin, jun. Efq.
—— Mairn, Efq.
Mrs. Miller.
Colonel Morgan.
Charles Monro, Efq.
Q. M.
Henry Mills, Efq.
Robert Mangles, Efq.

N.
Dutchefs of Northumberland.
Countefs Dowager of Northampton.
The Hon. Mrs. North.
Mrs. Norman.
Mrs. Nichols.
William Nedham, Efq.
Mrs. Newland.
Thomas Newnham, Efq.
Mr. Newton.
James Nutt, Efq.
Mr. Nefbitt.
Frederic Naffau, Efq.
Mrs. Nichols.
Rev. Mr. Newbolt.
Francis Newbery, Efq.
Richard Neave, Efq.

James Neave, Efq.
Richard Norman, Efq.
Mrs. R. Norman.
George Norman, Efq.
R. N. Neville, Efq.
Mifs Neville.
Mrs. Norman, Henley.

O.
Hon. Mrs. Olmius.
Mr. Opie.
Mrs. Opie.
John Ouvery, Efq.
Mrs. Onflow, Dover-Street.
John Orde, Efq.
Mrs. Orde.

P.
Countefs of Portfmouth.
Lord Vifcount Peterfham.
Lord Pelham.
Lady Pelham.
Rt. Hon. Lady C. Peachy.
Hon. Mr. Pelham.
Hon. Thomas Pelham.
Hon. Philip Pufey.
Hon. Henry Pelham.
—— Papillon, Efq.
Mifs Papillon.
Rev. Mr. Papillon.
Mr. Parkinfon.
Mifs Park.
Mifs Puggin.
Mrs. Pattifon.
Mrs. Pott.

Mifs

Mifs Porter.

Mifs S. Papillon.

The Rev. Mr. Pettingal.

Colonel Pownall.

John Pownall, Efq. .

P. L. Pownall, Efq.

Mrs. Pownall.

Mifs Pownall.

Mrs. P. Pownall.

Mr. Paynter.

Mrs. Peck.

Samuel Phipps, Efq. Lincoln's-Inn.

Mifs Pope.

Mifs S. Pope.

Arthur Pott, Efq.

Robert Pott, Efq.

Mrs. Robert Pott.

William Morton Pitt, Efq.

Mrs. Morton Pitt.

Mrs. Paulhan.

Mifs Partridge.

Mr. Potts.

Mr. Peppin.

Mr. Pulsford.

Mr. Park.

Mrs. Prefcot.

James Leigh Perrot, Efq.

Mrs. Leigh Perrot.

Mrs. Platel.

Mrs. Piggot.

Mrs. Pottinger.

Mrs. Powlett.

Mrs. Pollen.

Mifs Pierce.

William Prefcot, Efq.

Richard Prefcot, Efq.

Mrs. Peck.

—— Piele, Efq.

Mr. Pearfon, Serle-Street.

Mrs. Palmer.

Dr. Prendergaft.

Mrs. Payne.

Rev. Charles Powlett, jun.

William Powlett Powlett, Efq.

Thomas Norton Powlett, Efq.

Mrs. Charles Powlett.

Mrs. Price.

Sir J. Peachy, Bart.

Mifs Pyott.

Sir Ferdinando Poole, Bart.

Rev. Henry Poole.

Thomas Partington, Efq.

John Purling, Efq.

John Pratt, Efq.

Mrs. Parker, Chancery-Lane.

Q.

Mrs. Quick.

Mrs. Quintin.

R.

The Bifhop of Rochefter.

Countefs of Rothes.

Lady Ravenfworth.

Lady Rivers.

—— Raycroft, Efq.

Mrs. Robarts.

George Richards, Efq.

Mifs Rayne.

Auguftus

Auguſtus Rogers, Eſq.
Mrs. Rogers.
John Robinſon, Eſq.
Mrs. Raper, Hertford-Street.
Thomas Ryder, Eſq.
Mrs. Robinſon.
Morris Robinſon, Eſq.
George Robinſon, Eſq.
Mrs. Robinſon, Buxfield.
Mrs. Ring.
Miſs M. Ring.
Mrs. Ryder.
Rev. Mr. Raſhleigh.
Mrs. Rivers.
Mr. Richards.
Rev. Sir Peter Rivers, Bart.
Lady Rivers.
Mrs. Rolleſtone.
Rev. Mr. Reynel.
Thomas Richardſon, Eſq.
Thomas Raikes, Eſq.
Mrs. Raikes.
George Roſe, Eſq.
John Randall, Eſq.
Rev. Mr. Roſe.
Charles Raikes, Eſq.

S.
The Hon. Lincoln Stanhope.
Lady Shelly.
Sir John Skinner.
Lady Skinner.
Rev. Dr. Sturges, Chancellor of Wincheſter.

Mrs. Smith.
Mrs. Scotlowe.
Mrs. T. Scotlowe.
Mrs. Sober.
Miſs Sober.
Miſs Savary.
Mrs. Snelling.
Mrs. Strode.
Sir John Stepney, Bart.
Mr. Simmons.
Miſs Stanton.
Launcelot Shadwell, Eſq.
Miſs Sampſon.
James Sibbald, Eſq.
Matthew Smith, Eſq.
Mr. Steele.
Mrs. Shuttleworth.
Mrs. Snell.
Mr. Sowerby.
Mr. Satherthwaite.
Mr. Secretan.
Miſs Sproule.
Miſs Skinner.
———— Stonhewer, Eſq.
Miſs Simpſon.
Mrs. Spry.
Mrs. Stafford.
T. Manners Sutton, Eſq.
Mrs. Simeon.
Mr. E. B. Simonds.
Mrs. Smart.
Mr. John Stevens.
Miſs Ann Stow.
Benjamin Sidey, Eſq.

John

John Scott, Efq.
William Selwyn, Efq.
Mr. William Smith.
Mr. Sharp.
—— Stiles, Efq.
Mr. T. Sewell, Cornhill.
Mrs. Seymour.
The Rev. Mr. Shorland.
Mifs Mary St. John.
Mr. Smith.
Mrs. Smith.
Richard Vernon Sadleir, Efq.
Richard Stone, Efq.
Jofhua Smith, Efq.
Mrs. Smith.
Samuel Shergold, Efq.
Charles Scrafe, Efq.
John Stables, Efq.

T.

Mifs Turner.
Mifs Jane Turner.
The Rt. Hon. Lady Frances Tal-
mafh.
The Hon. Charles Townfend.
Mrs. Tillard.
Mrs. M. Townfhend.
Mrs. Thompfon.
Mifs Theed.
Mrs. Sutton Turquand.
Sutton Turquand, Efq.
Mrs. Tom.
Mrs. Turquand.
Mrs. Thornton.

John Trevanion, Efq.
Mrs. Trevanion.
The Rev. John Tickel.
Mrs. Tickel.
The Rev. Mr. Trickey.
Mrs. Trimbrell.
Lady Taylor.
Afhton N. Toll, Efq.
Mr. George Booth Tindale.
William Trollope, Efq.
Mr. Richard Twining.
Mr. John Twining.
John Toke, Efq.
Stephen Teffier, Efq.
Peter Thelluffon, Efq.
Mrs. Thelluffon.
Richard Tidy, Efq.
—— Taylor, Efq.

V.

Unknown by G. G.
Lord Vernon.
Lady Vernon.
Unknown.
Unknown.
Robert Udny, Efq.
Mr. O. Vincent.
Rev. Richard Valpey.
J. Vernon, Efq. Lincoln's-Inn.
J. Vernon, jun. Efq.
Mifs Vernons.
Mr. Vines.
Mrs. Udny.
Mifs Vernon.

Mifs

Mifs Elizabeth Vernon.
William Vaughan, Efq.

W.

Earl of Warwick.
Countefs of Warwick.
Lord Wallingford.
Rev. Dr. Wollafton.
Captain Weir, Wickham, Hants.
Mrs. Weir.
Jofeph Warner, Efq.
Mrs. Warner.
Hutton Wood, Efq.
William Webber, Efq.
William Webber, junior, Efq.
Mrs. Wefton.
Dr. Willis.
Mrs. Whilom.
Mifs Walker.
Mr. Juftice Wilfon.
Mr. Warington.
Mrs. Willgrefs.
Samuel Worrall, Efq. Clifton.
Samuel Worrall, junior, Efq.
Mr. George Worrall.
Mifs Worrall.
Abraham Winterbottom. Efq.
Mrs. Wilkinfon.
Mifs Wilkinfon.
Robert Walpole, Efq.
Robert Walpole, junior, Efq.
Thomas White, Efq.
Mr. R. White.
Mrs Weftern.

Mifs Weftern.
Mr. Wood.
Mr. Ward.
Mrs. Which.
Mr. Withers.
Mr. Wills.
Mrs. Weddell.
Elbro. Woodcock, Efq.
Mrs Woodcock.
The Rev. Mofes Wight.
The Rev. O. Wight.
Thomas Walfham, Efq.
Mrs. Walfham.
Mifs Watfon.
Mrs. Webb, Binfield.
Mifs Webb.
Mrs. Weft.
John Wilmot, Efq.
Mrs. Walker.
Mrs. Warren.
Mrs. Williams.
Mrs. Watfon.
Hankin Wall, Efq.
John Wells, Efq.
William Wells, Efq.
Mr. Willis.
Mr. Wormald.
Mr. J. Wormald.
William Walcot, Efq.
J. W. Efq.
Rev. Thomas Warton.
The Rev. Dr. Warton, Prebendary
of Winchefter.
Mrs. Warton.

c

Mrs.

Mrs. Wray.

Mr. Winter.

Mrs. J. Warre.

Mrs. M. Woodford

Mr. Walker.

Rev. Mr. Webfter.

Rev. Mr. Whalley.

Mrs. Wainwright, Hatton-Street.

Y.

Mrs. Young.

Lady Yates.

Mifs Young.

Mifs E. Young.

Mifs S. Young.

Timothy Yeates, Efq.

Rev. Charles Yalden.

THE

SORROWS of WERTER.

LETTER I.

WERTER to ******.

CONTENT and Peace have rear'd their quiet cell

Within the fhades of Walheim's fair retreat :

Charm'd with their fmiles, which know to charm fo well,

Here, oh my friend, I fix my ruftic feat.

B

Here

Here will I dwell beneath their gentle fway,

Beneath yon branching olive's friendly fhade :

Welcome the calm thefe heavenly guefts convey !

Fair as their forms, but, ah !—as foon to' fade.

Happy, thrice happy, whofe untainted mind

Delights to tafte the pleafures of the plain ;

Meets ftill enjoyment with retirement join'd,

Nor fcorns the paftimes of the lowly fwain.

Soft on his fenfes breathes the fragrant May,

Divinely radiant breaks the golden morn :

Pure are his joys which bloffom into day ;

His humble rofes bloom without a thorn.

Whilft

Whilſt I in theſe delights my hours emplo

Ah, let not ſlander wound thy Werter's name;

Dead to the world, I aſk no worldly joy;

If free from cenſure, I regard not fame.

The glorious wreath of war let others wear;

I ſeek not honours, wealth, or martial praiſe:

To pleaſe one charming maid be all my care:

Be hers the ſkill to mark my artleſs lays.

Yes, be it hers, ſecure in beauty's power,

With ſmiles to chaſe her doubtful lover's ſighs;

With ſweet diſcourſe to charm each happy hour,

The ſoul of virtue beaming from her eyes.

Ah,

Ah, where w███e's unbounded paſſion lead

This ardent flame?—ah, whither does it tend?

To Charlotte all my fervent vows are paid ;

To her my daily oriſons aſcend.

LETTER II.

TO THE SAME.

I BREATHE delight from Recollection's power,

Recalling days to me for ever gone:

Fled is the tender joy, the focial hour;

And I, alas! am left to figh alone.

Hope gayly led me to Elyfium's height,

The unknown profpect Fancy painted fair:

But, ah! too boldly daring was the flight!

For Difappointment lurk'd in ambufh there.

There

There midft ⬤ling woods fhe kept her feat

Where flowers luxuriant fcatter'd fragrance round;

Too carelefs I approach'd her clofe retreat:

Deep in my haplefs heart fhe fixt the wound.

Such is our fate, my friend, my hope's betray'd;

Yet, oh! my heart, the mutmuring figh reftrain:

'Tis Heaven's high will, and be that will obey'd;

Nor thou, poor injur'd fufferer, complain.

Life's faireft bloffoms only bloom to die;

For one fhort morn rejoice in pleafure's fun:

Chill evening comes—Ah, fee, they withering lie!

Ah, fee! how foon their courfe of beauty's run.

Alas!

Alas! my friend, whence fprings this fudden gloom?

Shall Albert's prefence fhade the fmiling day?

Yes, yes; this favour'd lover feals my doom;

This deftin'd hufband bears my peace away.

L E T-

LETTER   III.

TO   THE   SAME.

WRITTEN ON WERTER'S RETURN FROM WAL-
HEIM TO THE CITY.

H O W fad, alas! how cheerlefs is my ftate!

Like fome poor exile am I doom'd to rove;

Cut off from hope, abandon'd to my fate,

Expell'd from friendfhip, banifh'd far from love.

Thy voice no longer, with affection's powers,

Sooths the keen anguifh of my troubled breaft;

Fled are thofe days, thofe fond remember'd hours,

The hours of friendfhip, once fupremely bleft.

Yes,

Yes, they are fled, and I, alas! remain

A lonely outcaft midft encircling joys;

Conftrain'd to mingle with the idly vain,

Whofe cold indifference all my blifs deftroys.

For, ah, how few from pleafure's paths will ftray,

To trace the fource whence inborn forrows flow!

Let them but trifle life's fhort hours away;

They care not for the pangs my heart may know.

Vain, empty world, thy boafted good how frail!

Thou, rigid fchool of mifery and cares!

The happieft find thee but a chequer'd vale,

And oh! how many more a vale of tears!

C

Where

Where facred Friendfhip ferves, a polifh'd mafk

To veil Hypocrify's diftorted mien;

Where bright illufions in the funbeams bafk,

And men and manners are not what they feem.

Ah, did no dangers meet our feeble eyes,

How calmly fmooth were Nature's fair extent!

But rocks meet rocks, on mountains mountains rife,

And man muft labour o'er the fteep afcent.

Yes, life's gay morning finks in evening's gloom,

The jealous clouds o'erhang the radiant light:

Content's fweet rofes feldom live to bloom,

Or know perfeftion on ambition's height.

2   Our

Our joys we meafure by a moment's fpace,

By ages reckon when diftrefs invades:

Panting and breathlefs run foft pleafure's race;

Wearied with pain, lie down or feek the fhades.

Oh, Death! thy deepeft fhades around me fpread;

Would, would, thy axe were levell'd at the tree!

Would that in death were laid this weary head!

For light and life have now no joys for me.

Thou great Supreme, enthron'd on mercy's fhrine,

Oh, hear, and bear me to thy peaceful fhore!

Joys undiminifh'd in thy prefence fhine,

" At thy right hand are pleafures evermore."

LET-

LETTER IV.

WERTER to CHARLOTTE.

WRITTEN FROM A COTTAGE WHERE HE HAD TAKEN SHELTER FROM A STORM.

Escap'd from scenes where noise and folly dwell,

From senseless mirth, heart-rending tumult free;

Beneath this humble roof, this moss-grown cell,

I feel again restor'd to love and thee.

The snow descends, and thickens on the ground:

The winds against this peaceful shelter beat:

Yet while the storm is wild and loud around,

How sweet the calm that dwells in this retreat!

In

In this lone fpot, midft thefe fequefter'd fhades,

Thy image, Charlotte, preffes on my foul;

Thy heavenly mildnefs every fenfe pervades,

Thy winning graces all my powers control.

Thus ever banifh'd from my Charlotte's fight,

The pooreft wretch on earth may pity me:

What is this life?—a tedious winter's night:

Ah! what my ftate, renounc'd by Heaven and thee?

Why were thofe times, o'er which my memory ftrays,

Why were they once fo fortunate and fair?

'Twas that my grateful foul with humble praife

Refign'd to Providence each anxious care.

Still

Still that fame Providence benignant reigns;

Creation fmiles, unnumber'd worlds adore:

" Nature ftill charms the fenfe of happier fwains;"

But, ah! my heart can tafte her charms no more!

All, all is paft. Here wild Diforder reigns:

Each focial joy from me for ever gone;

The tyrant Love now holds my heart in chains,

And Reafon abdicates her falling throne.

How fweet was once to me the early dawn!

Not to the lark more welcome was the fun:

" I fprang to meet him on the upland lawn,"

And thought his daily courfe too fwiftly run.

Now

Now tow'rds the weſtern hills he creeps ſo ſlow;

I loath the ſun, and chide his ſluggard pace:

When morn returns—alas, it quickens woe:

Oh! might I ſink again in ſleep's embrace!

"Sleep, like the world, its ready viſits makes

"Where Fortune ſmiles," where the horizon's clear;

"Swift on its downy" wings the wretch forſakes,

"And lights on lids unſullied with a tear."

Ah, pitying Heaven! yet again reſtore

Thoſe golden days when hope was in its prime:

Ye tender hours of love return once more,

Return and loiter to the end of time.

Oh!

Oh! that my fum of days, of months, and years,

Had all been crowded in that little fpace!

Or could, alas! my fighs, and ftreaming tears,

All thoughts, but thofe of happy love efface!

Why muft I to ambitious hopes refort?

Why join the bufy crowd, or madly go

Where Pleafure's fons in gay profufion fport,

And tafte no joys but what from pleafure flow?

Ah, happier far an humble fwain to dwell,

Bleft with thy fmiles, in this fecure retreat!

With fond delight of forrows paft to tell,

To breathe my fervent paffion at thy feet.

Ah,

Ah, no, my Charlotte, midft the city's gloom,

Chain'd to the oar, I yet muft act my part :

To mix with ftrangers is my wretched doom ;

Strangers indeed to this devoted heart.

Methinks I live within a vaft machine !

A pageant there whofe ftrong deception charms ;

Where Folly governs ftill each varying fcene,

And the light puppets bound to her alarms.

Amus'd, infected, midft the dazzling glare,

Awhile I fported in the myftic fhew :

Till the firft hand I touch'd, though feeming fair,

I felt was wood—I fhrunk—and mine withdrew.

D

Ye

Ye airy flutterers in a fummer's fun,

Who glide like morning vapours from the fight;

Say, were ye born to fill thofe fcenes alone

Whofe paths are ftrew'd with rofe-buds of delight?

Ye fportive race round Diffipation's fhrine,

Think—will not Time avenge his wafted hour?

Shall he not come in majefty divine,

Come, at the laft, array'd in awful power?

Ah! what is *laft*? Juft Heaven! that word confounds

My prefent fenfe, perplexes all the paft:

My weak conceptions ftrike not with its founds,

Not one idea will accord with *laft*.

That

That Power fupreme, who mark'd the deftin'd line

Beyond whofe bounds no human eye extends,

Was pleas'd, fo dim our day of life fhould fhine,

We fcarce can trace where it begins or ends.

Dark hang the clouds of life's unhappy day,

With darker ftorms of forrow yet to come:

Weary and fickening Fancy dies away,

While Hope almoft expires upon her tomb.

Fainting fhe lifts her clofing eyes above,

And points my wifhes to a happier fhore;

To the pure fountain of eternal love,

Where Care's pale image fhall intrude no more.

The

The fun is funk beneath the weſtern ſky,

The moon begins her empire to aſſume:

Time warns me from this peaceful ſcene to fly,

Alas! it warns me to my priſon's gloom.

While Albert—Ah, too lovely Charlotte, ſay!

Say! haſt thou crown'd him ſovereign of thy fate?

Haſt thou?—Yet, oh! the dreaded truth delay,

'Tis Werter's ſentence—can it come too late?

LETTER V.

CHARLOTTE to WERTER.

AH, reſtleſs mortal!—had I bid thee die,

And bathed the mandate with my flowing tears,

Then hadſt thou bleſt me with thy parting ſigh,

Hadſt died a martyr to unmanly fears.

But when I ſooth thy pains, and bring relief;

To hope and peace direct thy drooping views;

Canſt thou then yield, ſo poorly yield to grief,

And all my fond ſolicitude refuſe?

Oh!

Oh! I can feel, too exquifitely feel ;

This heart too near to feeling is allied :

Yet would I veil, its fweeteft charms conceal,

Ere they fhould Reafon's better judgment guide.

Yes, I can weep ; fad fympathy is mine :

But is that friendfhip worth the pitying tear,

Which feeks on Sorrow's bofom to recline,

And falls a willing victim to Defpair ?

Friendfhip has hopes which light a brighter flame,

Hopes I will cherifh with a fond delight :

Chafe then her fears, thofe foes to honeft fame,

And give Activity her fcope for flight.

Oh,

Oh, Werter! fhake this palfy from thy mind:

Yet rife fuperior to depreffion's power:

Still let defeat, with patient courage join'd,

Rival the glory of the victor's hour.

Seek not the gloomy confines of defpair,

The dreary caverns of defponding wiles:

Ceafe with the world to wage unequal war,

Nor turn indignant from her offer'd fmiles.

This world's injuftice man has oft arraign'd;

Complaining ftill while privileg'd to live:

Learn to defpife the injury fuftain'd;

And with a Chriftian charity forgive.

The

The hour of death is haften'd or delay'd

By him alone who beft difcerns our good :

Ceafe then, ah ceafe, his wifdom to upbraid,

Too oft arraign'd, too little underftood.

LETTER VI.

WERTER to ******.

WRITTEN ON A VISIT TO THE PLACE OF HIS BIRTH.

WHILST with the fervour of a pilgrim's zeal

On thefe my native plains I fondly ftand,

More foft emotions o'er my fenfes fteal

Than meet the faint within the holy land.

Whilft with his zeal I view thefe hallow'd bowers,

How does the well-known profpect charm my foul!

My heart expands beyond expreffion's powers;

Beyond the force of reafon to control.

E   When

When at the clofe of each declining day,

Marking the object of my wifhes nigh,

Through the long vale I homeward bent my way,

The welcome cottage met my longing eye.

" My dog, the faithful guardian of its gate,"

With eager hafte to greet his mafter flew ;

The favourite fubject of my little ftate,

By love diftinguifh'd from the chofen few.

Ah, ftealing Time ! full many a paffing year

Has lightly floated with thy rapid tide,

Since Fortune drew me from this humble fphere,

O'er dangerous heights my fanguine fteps to guide.

Oh !

Oh! how thefe fcenes recal each happy hour,

Each fond endearment fafe by memory ftor'd!

Safe from the ftretch of Fortune's fickle power,

Lock'd in thefe groves fo blooming, fo ador'd.

Behold where, planted by thefe partial hands,

The rofes mingled with the woodbines grow!

Behold where yonder weeping willow ftands!

Hail, thou fad emblem of poor Werter's woe!

Where'er I paufe, and, penfive, look around,

Remembrance wakens all her bufy train;

Here fportive childhood lightly prefs'd the ground;

Here once did Pleafure hold her golden reign.

Here

Here would fhe loiter by the tinkling rill,

Or gayly tripping o'er the cowflip bed,

Gaze with delight on yonder bufy mill :

Thefe were her haunts, but thefe, alas ! I fled.

Oh, ever dear Remembrance ! guide my way

Through the lov'd mazes of each youthful fcene :

Thou too, gay Fancy, hither freely ftray ;

Come, thou delufive, vifionary queen.

Come, let us range the verdant meads along,

Thofe feats of carelefs innocence and eafe ;

Retrace once more, the fportive vales among,

Thofe tender years when every fport could pleafe.

Sweet

Sweet to the fenfe arofe the fanning gale,

Whilft fweeter bloffoms fcatter'd fragrance wide :

Simplicity adorn'd the lonely dale,

With white-rob'd Decency, her modeft guide.

Youth's fprightly morn its genial influence fhed,

Fondly exulting in the years to come ;

Health's ruddy grace thefe glowing cheeks o'erfpread,

While fmiling Pleafure dimpled in their bloom.

Ye lofty pines encircling yonder towers ;

Ye cryftal ftreams that murmur as ye flow ;

Ye verdant plains, ye ever facred bowers,

Ah, why did I your chafte delights forego ?

How

How oft beneath yon fpreading walnut's fhade

The term, the object of my bounded view,

In happy ignorance I carelefs laid,

Fixt on a world I then fo little knew!

How on that world did Expectation lean,

In brighteft colours painting every charm;

Whilft Fancy's glow ftill rais'd the dazzling fcene,

How did its glare my youthful bofom warm!

Bane to my peace! the phantom I purfued;

But, oh! too foon the fatal change I mourn'd:

From that ideal world fo fondly view'd,

Ye halcyon fhades, how loft am I return'd!

Sweet

Sweet peace of mind, oh, whither art thou fled?

From thy pure fource fhall joys no longer flow?

Muft Difappointment raife her hydra head,

And every fancied blifs prove real woe?

Alas! how foon the flowers of life decay!

Bloom with the morn, and with the evening clofe!

Or fhould they yet furvive a longer day,

How little fruit to fair perfection grows!

Why of that little are we then profufe?

Why caft with lavifh hand its bloom away?

For oh, my friend! ere well we mark its ufe,

The faireft fruit is haftening to decay.

Such

Such is the deftiny of man on earth,

Awhile he's borne on Hope's expanded wing;

Fair as the bud his tender youth puts forth

In all the foft luxuriance of fpring.

But fee! th' indignant fky unfriendly lowers,

See! blafts deftructive poifon young defire;

Wait but the change of fome few fleeting hours,

And all his hopes, his promis'd joys expire.

Ye fylvan fhades, here could I ever reft!

Yet I again muft leave your peaceful plains;

Again return, to be again diftrefs'd;

Thus ftern Ambition holds the world in chains.

Yet

Yet 'tis not pomp, nor prouder learning's force,

Can mark our deftiny in future fate;

No, 'tis the *mind*; from whence derives its fource

Each virtuous deed, whate'er is good and great.

I prize that *mind* beyond or wealth, or fame;

Beyond what knowledge, or what arts beftow:

'Tis my fond boaft: It is my only claim:

The worth of knowledge all with me may know.

But ah, vain boaft! its faireft claim is loft!

A wounded temper fickens in diftafte:

By love undone, by difappointment croft,

My mind is now, alas! a ruin'd wafte.

Why

Why was I mark'd love's haplefs pangs to know?

Why muft my heart in ceafelefs anguifh groan?

That heart which bled at each recited woe,

How fhall its tender frame endure its own?

Oh, thou all glorious Sun who rul'ft the day!

Unchang'd fince firft the race of time began;

In quick fucceffion haftening to decay,

Thou haft beheld the fleeting life of man.

One generation hails thy cheering light,

Then faft declining, as a fhadow fpeeds;

Another rifing finks again in night,

And ftill another in its turn fucceeds.

Alas,

Alas, bright orb! there yet will come a day,

Stupendous thought! when thou no more ſhalt riſe:

The globe itſelf ſhall then diffolve away ;

Thick darkneſs cover earth, and veil the ſkies.

That word which form'd the world, that powerful word

Again ſhall ſhake this univerſal frame :

But thou ſhalt never change, Almighty Lord!

Eternal Father! Thou art ſtill the ſame.

LETTER VII.

WERTER to CHARLOTTE.

IN vain I feek from change of place to find

A change to thought; an antidote to care:

Still this unhappy, felf-deftroying mind

With cruel energy purfues me there.

In vain I feek by abfence to remove

Thy beauteous form imprefs'd upon my heart:

Love ftill triumphant, all fubduing Love

Derides my flight, and claims the conqueror's part.

Why

Why then, ah, wherefore fhould I wand'ring mourn

A wretched fugitive from pole to pole?

No—like the patriarch's dove will I return

To thee, my Charlotte, magnet of my foul.

LETTER VIII.

WERTER to ******.

TORTUR'D in abfence, hopelefs of relief,

I feek thofe fhades from whence fo late I came;

With vain regret, and fond enduring grief,

Like fome poor moth, I hover round the flame.

So weak is man, his beft refolves fo frail,

So fhort the date of Reafon's boafted fway;

When Paffion, Love, or Folly's varying gale

Shall fweep the mental monitor away!

The

The ſtricken deer with ſighs and ſhortening breath

Seeks thro' ſequeſter'd wilds and paths to go:

Thus I, alas! invoking Peace and Death,

Unpitied bear my ſolitary woe.

Thy groves, oh Walheim! bloom with peace alone,

For Charlotte conſecrates thy ſweet retreat:

There will I dwell unknowing and unknown,

There caſt my mournful numbers at her feet.

There from the world, and all its follies free,

With many a pang of hopeleſs love oppreſt,

This throbbing boſom, like a troubled ſea,

Huſh'd to a calm, ſhall rock itſelf to reſt.

L E T-

LETTER IX.

TO THE SAME.

THE clock proclaims in flow and solemn strains

A long farewel to the departing year ; ·

One hour alone, one little hour remains—

Reflection whispers what I blush to hear.

Oh ! let me seize the moments ere they fly,

For all our fleeting years shall quickly end :

Swift as they pass then, I'll the hours apply

To contemplation, reason, and my friend.

Time,

Time, like the filent plunderer of night,

Makes on our little hoard fome hourly theft;

Shall we then, dazzled by life's glaring light,

Hope to endure till of each hope bereft?

The tree, when ftripp'd by hoary Winter's hand,

Again may bloom, again rich foliage bring;

The grafs which dies, and naked leaves the land,

Again revive with the returning fpring.

But man, weak man, his tranfient feafon o'er,

Falls to be mingled with his kindred clay;

In duft he flumbers to awake no more,

Till earth and heaven fhall diffolve away.

G   Thou-

Thoufands are cherifh'd but to breathe and die;

So near allied the cradle and the tomb.

Thoufands who live, but live to infamy,

Degrade exiftence, and provoke their doom.

Yet Heaven is juft, eternal goodnefs fure :

Unerring Wifdom ftamps each fair defign.

Oh! let us then with humble hope endure,

Revere his will, nor impioufly repine.

Alas! the change a few fhort months have made!

How fwiftly is my youthful vigour flown!

Sloth and dull lethargy my powers invade,

And all the energy of life is gone.

Nature's

Nature's fweet afpect can delight no more ;

No more her charms re-animate this frame :

The dazzling world's refplendency is o'er,

The fun's bright luftre is no more the fame.

Where then, ah, where is life's attractive charm,

That active fpring whofe nervous force impels ?

Farewel at once to hope's delufive calm !

When peace no longer centres in ourfelves.

Hard 'tis to combat with the ocean's tide,

But harder ftill 'gainft paffion's force to move :

Come then, my friend, this fhatter'd veffel guide,

And fave it from the dangerous rocks of love.

LET-

L E T T E R X.

W E R T E R TO A L B E R T.

ON HIS MARRIAGE.

HAIL, Albert! hail! may bleſſings wait my friend!

The beſt of bleſſings in thy charming bride!

Oh! may propitious Heaven thy blifs extend,

And grant thee every good, to me denied!

Night's gloomy horrors darken all my ſoul;

Reſtleſs I dream, I rave, and wildly ſtart:

Repoſe ſtill flies, difdainful of control;

No hope enlightens now my cheerleſs heart.

Deſpair,

Defpair, and woe, and wild diftraction reigns;

I droop and wither in life's early bloom:

I ftruggling figh to break thefe galling chains,

And fink to peaceful flumber in the tomb.

Be Werter's forrows all forgotten there,

Save, that remembrance lives in Charlotte's heart—

Ah, yet allow me in that heart to fhare,

To fhare with thee, at leaft, foft pity's part.

Oh, Albert, Albert! make that angel bleft;

So may domeftic joys around thee dwell!

While I, an outcaft, loft to peace and reft,

To thee and Walheim bid a long farewell.

LET-

LETTER XI.

WERTER to * * * * * *.

—" I MUST depart."——Ah, my prophetic friend!

How apt the phrafe, how fitted to my heart!

Yes—'tis refolv'd—thy fummons I attend;

Better, far better 'tis, I fhould depart.

But not to liften to ambition's lore,

Nor yet thro' folly's beaten paths to ftray;

Now do I haften tow'rds a calmer fhore—

My chofen journey points a fafer way.

And

And wilt thou come my doubtful courfe to fteer ?

Wilt thou repair thy weary friend to meet ?

Yet paufe awhile : thy promis'd aid defer

Till next my pen thy friendly care fhall greet.

Pluck not the fruit too early from the fpray,

Ere the meridian fun mature its bloom :

Another week, perchance another day,

May fill the ripening clufter's rich perfume.

Another day,—and fate's dire web is fpun :

My foul grows fick, tir'd Nature feeks repofe :

Ere the next dawn of yon declining fun

Thefe eyes to life, and all its ills, fhall clofe.

6   But,

But, oh! maternal anguiſh wrings my heart:

A mother's ſorrows agonize my breaſt.

Ah! haſte my friend, and with each ſoothing art

Calm thou the mourner's troubled ſoul to reſt.

Implore a bleſſing on her parting ſon,

Move her to pity, to forgiveneſs move:

Sure I was born to weigh deſtruction down,

And heap diſtreſs on all I fondly love.

Full is the meaſure of poor Werter's woes;

Thou rapid tide of grief, ah, ceaſe to ſwell!

Alas! my cup of bitterneſs o'erflows:

Yet—peace my ſoul—for all may yet be well.

" Peace

" Peace fits on high, and fmiling mocks mankind ;"

Oh, thou Supreme! I thank thee for the view;

Thank thee who gave to my diftracted mind

Thro' death the lovely phantom to purfue.

Yes, I'm prepar'd, I grafp the chilling fteel;

Farewel, my friend! may every joy be thine!

Or, if fome mingled forrows thou muft feel,

Oh, may thofe forrows never equal mine!

H   L E T-

LETTER XII.

WERTER to CHARLOTTE.

YES, I muft die—yes—it is fo decreed :
Thefe eyes fhall not behold to-morrow's fun.
Oh, my foul's treafure! oh, forgive the deed!
Charlotte is wed;—and Werter is undone.

Oh! hadft thou bleft me with a parting figh,
Hadft thou in pity breath'd one laft adieu ;
Though doom'd to fuffer, though refolv'd to die,
My foul had once more known where comfort grew.

Would,

Would, would, alas, life's tedious dream were o'er!

Would that thefe eyes were clos'd in peaceful reft!

Yes, my lov'd Charlotte, 'tis a dream, no more;

An idle dream which but deludes at beft.

Religion's facred truths my foul reveres;

Refpects the holy joys her laws impart:

That angel-voice which dries affliction's tears;

That godlike-hand which binds the broken heart.

Yet, oh! to death I fly a willing flave;

Hail the dread king, his icy fceptre fold:

Though trembling Nature fhudders at the grave,

So dark that awful grave,—fo deep,—fo cold.

Yes,

Yes, thou all-conquering power, to thee I fly—

Let thy cold bofom give my forrows room :

Wearied with life, 'tis happinefs to die :

Welcome the folemn filence of the tomb.

Ah, coward Nature I wherefore doft thou fear ?

Why cling fo clofe to life's tempeftuous fhore ?

Oh ! break the ten-fold cord which binds thee here,

And, wing'd with hope, to happier regions foar.

Far, far above yon diftant orbs afpire ;

For foon, my foul, unfetter'd fhalt thou be :

Yes, heavenly inmate, yes, thou vital fire,

I'll give thee freedom, if thou dar'ft be free.

Then

Then farewel hope! delufive fource of woe!

Defpair has arm'd me for a firmer part:

One painful ftruggle, one decifive blow,

Cures all the forrows of this bleeding heart.

Should'ft thou, my Charlotte, chance thy way to bend

Where oft delighted we together ftray'd;

Give all thy thoughts, thy forrows to a friend,

By love, alas! but not by thee, betray'd.

And when at eve the fun's declining rays

Gild the proud fummit of yon mountain's brow,

Think on thy Werter's once enraptur'd days;

Ah! think, my Charlotte, what is Werter now.

O'er

O'er each affecting fcene let memory rove ;

Trace back my foft attention, tender fears ;

Oh! let it paint a too impaffion'd love,

By broken fighs exprefs'd, or falling tears.

Yet, my lov'd Charlotte, yonder humble grave

Demands a tribute from thy ftreaming eyes.

See, to the wind thofe flender poppies wave,

And mark the fpot where wretched Werter lies.

May fome fond lines record thy lover's name ;

Let not his noble paffion lie conceal'd :

He boafts no honours ; love was all his fame ;

To future ages be that love reveal'd.

Yes,

Yes, thou wilt weep; thy tender heart will bleed

While thy flow fteps approach thy lover's tomb;

Yes, thou wilt reprobate the fatal deed;

But Charlotte's tears fhall confecrate his doom.

Thofe gentle tears outweigh the pomp of art,

" The blaze of heraldry," the trump of praife:

To reign one hour in that angelic heart,

Exceeds the proudeft trophies Fame could raife.

Oh! I was calm as evening's filent hours

When firft I touch'd upon this tender theme;

But fad remembrance wakens nature's powers,

And now my tears from bitter anguifh ftream.

Flow

Flow ye foft drops, as fummer dews defcend

Refrefhing earth, fo blefs my burning heart:

In its laft ftruggles all your foftnefs blend,

And footh, oh footh my foul ere it depart.

Alas! I am not mad; I do not rave:

No, Charlotte, while I breathe this laft adieu,

I fee exiftence dawn beyond the grave,

Exiftence in eternity with you.

Bleft be that hope, which gilds my parting day,

I'll hail the cherub with my lateft breath,

Whofe beam refulgent darts fo bright a ray,

It cheers the dreary path which leads to death.

Say !

Say! fhould fome prodigal repentant fon

Before his injur'd father's throne appear;

Fall on his neck, and own himfelf undone;

Would he not kifs away the confcious tear?

" Father forgive," he cries, " the fhameful deed;

" Forgive thy erring child yet once again :"—

Though there he ceafe, ftill Nature's voice fhall plead;

Oh, ye affections! can fhe plead in vain?

And wilt thou, heavenly Father, feal my woe,

Should I appear before the deftin'd time?

'Scap'd from my weary pilgrimage below,

Wilt thou expel me from thy heavenly clime?

When

When dumb confufion veils the timid eye;

When blufhing penitence thefe cheeks o'erfpread ;

Oh, thou Omnipotent ! who reign'ft on high,

Arm not thy thunders 'gainft this guilty head.

Thou, God ador'd ! almighty King of Heaven !

Mercy, eternal Lord ! is thine alone ;

Oh, thro' that mercy be my crime forgiven,

When I for judgment ftand before thy throne !

Charlotte farewel ! yet *we* fhall meet again ;

My mind grows calm—the dreadful ftruggle's o'er—

Farewel, thou world of mifery and pain !

Pafs one fhort hour, and—Werter is no more.

LETTER XIII.

CHARLOTTE to LOUISA.

THE scene is clos'd; hark! hark! yon awful bell!

Those solemn sounds the horrid act proclaim :

Why, my Louisa, do I live to tell?

Ah, why to tremble thus at Werter's name?

Where were ye fled in that distressful hour,

Ye guardians of our fate, angelic band?

Some dæmon sure usurp'd your sacred power,

Deceiv'd his heart, and arm'd his desperate hand.

Oh

Oh Werter! did fallacious Reason dare

Give strength or colour to the frantic deed?

Could such false glofs thy generous foul enfnare?

Could such delusion with thy mind succeed?

Could'ft thou renounce Religion's holy caufe?

The bright reward to fuffering Virtue given?

Could'ft thou break through the first of Nature's laws,

And brave the juftice of offended Heaven?

Mifguided youth! alas! what peaceful throne,

What crown of glory, or what fair applaufe,

Awaits the conduct of that rebel fon,

Who dares to trample on a father's laws?

A fon

A son committed by his awful word

To diftant regions for fome noble end ;

On whofe obedience to the fovereign Lord,

The future fate of thoufands may depend.

Say ! fhall he fly, nor manfully abide

When threat'ning dangers meet him on the way ?

Impell'd by paffion's force, urg'd on by pride,

Shall his example teach the reft to ftray ?

Tho' Virtue warn him from the guilty choice,

Tho' ftill fhe ftrive his erring fteps to guide ;

Shall he indignant flight the heavenly voice,

And thruft the gentle monitor afide ?

Shall

Shall he, regardlefs of the facred truft,

Defert his ftation in the doubtful ftrife?

Remember, man;—thy great Creator's juft:

Oh, dread the fentence of the Lord of life.

" My fon, I call'd not; whence this rude appeal?

" Say! is thy courfe on earth fo fwiftly run?

" Haft thou fulfill'd my will, and prov'd thy zeal?

" Ah, rather fay that will is left undone.

" Say, that, impatient of my chaftening hand,

" On bold prefumption's venturous pinions borne,

" Thou'ft leap'd my bounds, defied my loud command,

" And rafhly plung'd from whence there's no return?

" Straight

" Straight was the path, which mark'd thy deftin'd way,

" Direct as Truth's unerring line could guide ;

" I freely gave thee Faith's enlightening ray,

" And bade Religion o'er thy fteps prefide.

" I gave thee talents to diftinguifh right ;

" I gave thee hope, to point a happier home :

" My word refounded from the realms of light :

" Endure ; be firm ;—for thou fhalt overcome.

" Why then, ah why, haft thou renounc'd my care ?

" Why fought thy own eternal peace to wound ?

" Prepare for judgment, oh, my fon ! prepare

" To hear the trumpet's laft decifive found.

" When

" When proud prefumption claims to be forgiven,

" Demanding audience of an injur'd God,

" Tho' Mercy reign the attribute of Heaven,

" Still Juftice bears the fceptre and the rod."

That bell again! oh, how it wounds my heart!

The train moves on, by mourning Friendfhip led;

My tears will flow: e'en Albert bears his part,

Melts at the fight, and weeps for Werter dead.

Ill-fated youth! why, urg'd by wild defpair,

On death's cold pillow didft thou feek repofe?

To-morrow's dawn perhaps had met thee fair,

To-morrow's fun difpell'd impending woes.

3

Were

Were thefe the precepts thy Redeemer gave ?

Were thefe the precepts which he died to feal ?

Did his example point thee to the grave,

Or give thy rafhnefs fhadow of appeal ?

No ; in fubmiffion's lowly garb array'd,

Refign'd, obedient to the will of God,

Tho' tempted, fcorn'd, abandon'd, and betray'd,

The perfect ways of righteoufnefs he trod.

Not many a pain, nor many a mournful hour,

Not prefent fufferings, nor the thoughts of paft,

Could move his conftant mind, or fhake his power ;

He bore them all ; but triumph'd in the laft.

K   When

When the Eternal faid to man,—be free,

He gave the human mind a will to choofe;

Plac'd him on earth, endued with liberty,

And good and evil offer'd to his views.

Cloth'd him with fenfe exalted and refin'd,

And form'd his feelings with peculiar care :

He gave to Reafon empire o'er the mind,

And Confcience fixt as his vicegerent there.

He plac'd Salvation's helmet on his head,

The fword of Faith appointed to his hand;

Virtue's fair fhield before the champion fpread,

And arm'd for conqueft bid the warrior ftand.

Rank'd

Rank'd as the chosen soldier of his will,

What then, oh man! does he require of thee?

What, but his word with meeknefs to fulfil,

And make thy life with truth's fixt laws agree?

With all the hero then, await the hour

When tried obedience fhall be crown'd with praife:

Againft defertion God will point his power,

And all the thunder of his vengeance raife.

Turn then, oh man! this great tranfgreffion fhun:

Strip off from Vice the flimfy veil fhe wears:

Sure, from her ways we fhall affrighted run,

When fhe in full deformity appears.

K 2

Thou,

Thou, bleſt Religion! all my foul imprefs;

Increaſe my faith; my humble hope increaſe:

" Thy righteous ways, are ways of pleaſantneſs;"

Yes, thou bright Seraph! " all thy paths are peace."

Oh, Werter! how my wounded heart deplores

The once impatiently expected hour,

When death ſhould join us on immortal ſhores,

Safe from the reach of every human power!

Deluſive hope! ah, hold my haſty pen!

Alas! he's turn'd apoſtate to my views.

Yet, it may be—the righteous Judge of men

Will not to ſorrow's voice this boon refuſe.

To

To his fad tomb at evening I'll repair,

Kifs the cold ground where Werter's afhes lie:

Then, weeping, breathe to Heaven the fervent prayer,

That Werter yet may mercy find on high.

Yes, Charlotte's prayers fhall reach Compaffion's throne;

Her fighs to Truth's celeftial realms afcend:

Oh, may the humble facrifice atone

For the loft reafon of her defperate friend!

F I N I S.

www.ingramcontent.com/pod-product-compliance
Lightning Source LLC
Chambersburg PA
CBHW021414090426
42742CB00009B/1141